FAITH, OBEDIENCE, AND SACRIFICE... AS INSPIRED BY THE HOLY SPIRIT

by

V. D. Williams

DORRANCE PUBLISHING CO., INC.
PITTSBURGH, PENNSYLVANIA 15222

Dorrance Publishing Co., Inc.
701 Smithfield Street
Pittsburgh, PA 15222
Visit our website at *www.dorrancebookstore.com*

ISBN: 978-1-4349-1259-6
eISBN: 978-1-4349-3973-9

This book is dedicated to everyone who supported me in this enduring process, especially those from Atlanta, Georgia and Baltimore, Maryland; with a special dedication to my mother, my children, and my dear friend, Al-Freda and to my late sister Laverne Dixon, her son Corey, and my friend C. Denise Johnson, and all my friends who have gone on home before me...may they rest in peace.

The much awaited and anticipated...
Faith...
Obedience...
and
Sacrifice

By V.D. Williams

As inspired by THE HOLY SPIRIT

Table of Contents

Inspirational Acknowledgment

These persons have contributed to my growth in the faith. They have encouraged me in ways beyond explanation. Listening to their TV broadcasts and reading their literature and materials have inspired me tremendously. They are what I call confirmation through divine intervention that faith, obedience, and sacrifice were destined to be in your hands at this very moment.

May the love of Christ reign in you at all times; for greater is He that is in you…than he who is in the world.

Merline Carothers
Beth Moor
T.D.Jakes
Joel Osteen
Paula White
Joyce Myers
The late Bishop Leo K Ceaser
My Mother Tina Dixon

Acknowledgments

New mercies we see each day. The Lord giveth and the Lord taketh. Blessed be the name of the Lord. In this new year, the Lord is doing a new thing. I would like to thank the Holy Spirit for its guidance and instruction. I would like to thank Jesus for His cleansing power, and I would like to thank God for Jesus.

In addition, I would like to thank the trustees (inmate workers) and officers at the DeKalb County Jail from Jan. 08 thru April 08. They have no idea how much support they rendered during my sabbatical there. Also, I would like to thank the tall woman pharmacist with the glasses who told me my life will never be the same again. Lauren Duarte stated, "With the devil, you will always lose, but with Jesus, you will always win." The devil is notorious but Jesus is victorious.

Thanks go out to Officer Mims, whose discipline and caring enabled me to meet some wonderful persons who are still a part of my life. Roland, thanks for being such a wonderful and true friend. Lucille Weaver, I love you. Rev. M. Whittaker, thank you for being a wonderful and Christ-filled Pastor.

To the late Bishop Leo K. Caesar and the First Mt. Oliver F.W.B. Church of Baltimore, Md. And to the current pastor, Bishop Oscar Brown and First Lady Jackie Brown and the entire congregation: Thank you. To Rev. Dr. Cedric Utsey, 1st Lady Evonne H. Utsey, and the entire congregation of Nicodemus Baptist Church, thank you for your support and love. The names of everyone who inspired and touched my life and who helped me along the way are too numerous to name for fear of leaving someone out.

Amen?

Amen.

Last but never least: I thank my entire family both immediate and extended, my in-laws. All of ya have shown nothing but love.

Hello, Mother, Tina Dixon and all my children both paternal and biological. Thank you Johnnie E. Williams for being a great father to our children every step of the way.

To all my acquaintances, friends, and enemies: Thank you.

A special shout out to my very special friend, Ms. Al-Freda Dickerson. I thank my current Pastor, Rev. William Gray III, 1st Lady Candice Gray, and the entire congregation of St. Stephens A.M.E. Church of Essex, MD.

A Bible Overview (NIRV)
How to Read the Bible

The Bible is divided into two main parts:

The Old Testament and The New Testament

The Old Testament comes first. It tells the story of creation of the universe and how evil came to the world. Here, you will also find God's plan to take back complete control of His world.

The Old Testament contains four main parts consisting of thirty-nine books.

The four main parts are: Beginnings, History, Wisdom and Worship, and Prophecy

The thirty-nine books fall as follows:

Beginnings—five

History—twelve

Wisdom and Worship—five

Prophecy—seventeen

Most of the Old Testament tells the story of the people of Israel. God chose this nation to tell the rest of the world about Him. God promises to send a special person, called the Messiah. He would make things right for all of us again. The Old Testament ends with Israel still waiting for the Messiah.

The New Testament begins with the coming of the Messiah—Jesus. You can read in the New Testament how Jesus came and lived on Earth. You will read about His pain and hurt while living in our troubled world. You will find what Jesus taught about life, love, and the coming of God's rule over the world.

The New Testament also tells us about Jesus' death and resurrection (how He rose from the dead). You can learn what this means for you and for the entire creation. Finally, you will read how the followers of Jesus should live until He comes back to make everything right.

The New Testament has three (3) main parts and twenty-seven books: History, Letters, and Prophecy

History—five

Letters—twenty-one

Prophecy—one

Each book of the Bible is made up of chapters.

The chapters have large numbers.

Each chapter is divided into verses (these are the smaller numbers).

To find a certain Bible passage, look up the page number for the book in the table of contents. Next, find the right chapter in the book by looking at the larger numbers on the pages. Finally, find the right verse by looking at the smaller numbers.

The Bible is filled with wonderful promises for your life. You will find wisdom, revelation, insight, light, direction, truth, love, compassion, and justice.

It contains the word of God, which is living and active. It is sharper than any sword that has two edges. It cuts deep enough to separate soul from spirit. It can separate joints from bones. It judges the thoughts and purposes of the heart (Hebrews 4:12).

The Bible tells you how to live in this world. Read it every day, from cover to cover and discover what's in it for you and what's in it for me (WII FM).

PEACE BE UNTO YOU.

Prologue

First, let me start off by saying, "Please accept my apology for taking so long to get this book to you." The Holy Spirit commissioned me to write this book in the fall of 2006 when I was ordained as an evangelist by Elder Cynthia Freeman.

At that time, the adversary was determined to stop God's work. But that, as you see, is impossible. The adversary slowed me down but, in the end, God will get the glory.

What blessings God has for you is for you. You will do what thus says the Lord. If the Holy Spirit has commissioned you to do a work for Him, then do it you will. If you have been blessed to experience a calling by the Father, you will do His will. Sometimes, it will take you to another place, which means leaving behind the people and things you love. But if you have **faith** in the Father, you will be **obedient** to His will, thus **sacrificing** what you must. His will *will* be done. He will provide something even more fulfilling at whatever destination He leads you to. I am a witness.

Remember Jonah in the belly of the fish? You cannot flee from the presence of the Lord (Psalm 139: 7-12v; Jonah 2:1-2v). Jonah prayed to the Lord his God from the fish's belly. And he said: "I cried out to the Lord because of my affliction, and He answered me… (Jonah 2: 6b). "Yet you have brought up my life from the pit, O LORD, my God…."

Thank you, Jesus. God will get the Glory.

The Lord kept me but denied me. He put me in the belly of the fish. I had no recourse but to do His will. He loves me and He loves you. The Holy Spirit isolated me and sanctified me so that His will could be done to His glorification.

Our God is sovereign. He can do whatever He wants when He wants anyway He wants.

In order to please God, we must have **faith**. Without **faith,** it is impossible to please God. In order to please God, you must be **obedient** to the Spirit. If you are guided by the Spirit, you won't fail to obey His word. In obeying His Word and keeping His commandments, you shall prosper wherever you go.

Obedience is better than sacrifice. For it is stated in Matthew 5:23-24, "Therefore if you bring your gift (sacrifice) to the altar and there remember that your brother has something against you, leave your gift (sacrifice) there before the altar, and go your way. First, be reconciled to your brother, and then come and offer your gift (sacrifice)." You cannot "buy" your way into the Kingdom. Be mindful to always give a portion of your first fruits, including your tithes and offerings that there may be food (meat) in the Lord's house. For "It is easier for a camel to go through the eye of a needle than for a rich man to enter the Kingdom of God," (Matthew 19:24).

Offer up the sacrifice of praise. For the sacrifices of God is a broken spirit. A broken and contrite heart—These, O God, You will not despise (Psalm 51:17).

For He gave us the Ultimate Sacrifice when He sent His son, Jesus. Our sacrifices were no longer valid. Our sins, transgressions, iniquities were too great. We were and still are filthy rags. We had to be clean in order for the Lord to accept us. No one, no, not one, was pure enough to be sacrificed for our sins. God could have done away with us, but He made us in His own image. His love for us is so great that He rendered the ultimate sacrifice, His Son. A great and last sacrifice, not of man nor beast, nor any manner of fowl; not a human sacrifice, but an infinite and eternal sacrifice. Their is not any man that can sacrifice his own blood to atone for the sins of another. That great and last sacrifice will be/had to be the Son of God (p.294 Aima 34:10-19 the book of Mormon)—And He shall bring salvation to all those who believe on His name—this being the intent of this last sacrifice, to bring about the bowels of mercy, which overpowereth justice and bringeth about means unto men that they may have **faith** unto repentance.

Begin to exercise your faith unto repentance, that you may began to call upon His Holy name, that He may have mercy upon you.

In addition, please humble yourselves and continue in prayer unto the Lord. Pray without ceasing over your household and against the power of your enemies who are against all righteousness. Pray to the Lord for your welfare and the welfare of those around you. Develop an intimate relationship with the Father, for it was the sacrifice of His Son that made intimate relationships possible.

Introduction

There is One God, One Faith, One Baptism

What you believe in is what you will have faith in. What you have **faith** in is what you will be **obedient** to, give glory to, praise to, and eventually honor. You will then begin to **sacrifice** your time, energy, and talents. You will give your monies and other forms of compensations. Your faith in what you love will cause you to trust in that which you have faith in. Think about it. No matter what your ethnicity, creed, race, gender is, there is still only One God (your Higher Power), One Faith (your Belief), and One Baptism (what you are Dedicated to).

If you are a child of God, this book will help you increase your faith, understand that you must be obedient to His Word, and in being obedient, you will make certain sacrifices and submit yourself to Christ; thus, improving your relationship with the Lord. We all need a closer walk and an intimate relationship with our Higher Power.

We must grow in faith as the Lord has given each of us a measure of faith. I am talking about a spiritual relationship with the Father, not a religious relationship. We all have our own religion in which either we have chosen, or it [religion] has been chosen for us, based on when and where we were born. Oftentimes, our adherence to a religion is often determined by the geographical locality of our birthplace. For instance, persons born in a socialist country over the last few decades may have no choice but to be raised an atheist (Gal. 1:13-14; Acts 23:6).

Through the enormous diversity of religious expressions found worldwide, man's search for God has led down many paths—from Hinduism to the monotheism of Judaism, Islam, and Christendom and to the Oriental philosophies of Shinto, Taoism, Buddhism, and Confucianism religious affiliation—all paths lead to one. Well, your religious affiliation is your prerogative. This book is more of a spiritual nature. It is geared toward aiding you, those who know the Lord, and those who want to know the Lord in acquiring a more intimate spiritual relationship with the Father.

Through faith, obedience, and sacrifice, you should gain a deeper understanding and enrich your knowledge in reference to communicating with the Father.

Faith-Related Bible Verses

John 3:16
John 20:29
Genesis 15:6
Isaiah 25:9
Isaiah 26: 3-4
Romans 12:3
Colossians 2:7
James 1:5-6
1Peter 1:7
Galatians 3:6-11
Hebrews 11
James 2:26
Heb. 12:2
1Tim 6:12
Eph 6:16
2Cor 5:7
Romans 3:22
Hab 2:4

Faith

How does faith affect our lives?

What do you believe in?

We trust in man (each other), but do you/we trust God???

With what/whom does your confidence and loyalty lie?

It is my hope and desire that the Lord Jesus Christ is the One with whom you have put your trust, confidence, loyalty, and faith in. It is He who rewards you daily in this life and the next—both internally and externally. I know it is difficult to trust the Lord when you are going through periods of sorrow and feeling lost and alone. Don't you know your feelings are unreliable? You are either going to trust in man or the Lord. Putting your trust in God will bring you all kinds of unexpected blessings. There is a certain peace within you when you rely on God daily.

Persons of various religious convictions rely on God daily—the just and the unjust, whether they are aware of it or not. To each person God has given a measure of faith (Rom 12:3). We exercise our faith knowingly and unknowingly. The more we exercise it, the more we grow in faith. However, faith without works is dead. There will come times in our life when we will get weary and distraught, wondering whether or not we are doing the right thing or making the right decision. It is times like these that we want to call on God. It is times like these we want to exercise our faith. It is times like these that we find out just how much faith we have. Have we done anything to cause our faith to grow in grace to the point that when we need our faith to work for us—we realize that we know that we know that we know? Or do you now question your relationship with God? Your faith is what connects you with God. Is it side by side or face to face? Is it just important or is it an intimate relationship with the Father?

By faith, we are saved through grace and not by ourselves. It is a gift. We must face it. In this day and time, we need the love of Christ. Times are getting worse. Bad habits are becoming harder to break. We need faith in our Lord because we need His aid in breaking bad habits. We can do no good thing alone. For when we think we can, believe me, the bad habit may come back worse than when it left (Or you merely thought it left.) Prayer changes things. Psalms 91:15 says, "Lord your word says that if I call on You, You will answer me; You will be with me in trouble. You will honor me and deliver me." I didn't say it...His Word says it.

As I stated, in this day and time, we need the love of Christ to sustain us. "Love works in much the same way as the force of faith. Faith is born into you when you are begotten of God. But until you began to act on God's word, that powerful force lies dormant. Faith becomes active through knowledge of the word," (p.77, *He did it All for You*, by Kenneth & Gloria Copeland).

Faith works by love. That which you love, you believe in. Where is your faith? What is your faith in? Have you thought about your faith? Faith is nurtured just as a baby is nurtured. There has to be a foundation, which is the basis of your faith. The foundation is important and necessary. It is the formative years of one's faith, just as a child's first five years are formative years. These years help determine how solid the foundation becomes. A solid foundation brings about a strong faith. The formation of the foundation directly has an enormous capacity. This directly affects one's behavior, behavior that will be obedient to God's word. Obedience comes from faith, which comes by hearing the word of God. One must listen. In order to listen, one must sacrifice one's time. Even if you don't understand "faith," believe in its power and you will start to feel the presence of the Holy Spirit directing you and talking to you. You will begin to see the manifestation of your faith, which will increase your trust in the Lord. As I stated earlier, God has dealt to each of us a measure of faith (Romans 12:3). Once you start to use what you have, the more your faith will grow.

Having and exercising your faith in God will help you to understand the Bible every time you pick it up to read. It contains every answer to every question. Use your faith prior to reading the Bible so that you understand what you are reading. How, you say...? By praying before reading. Everyone does not know how to read the Bible. Try understanding the "w" questions and finding out the answers to them first. Then you will find the revelations of reading the Bible fall into place. What do I mean by the "W" questions? I mean who, what, when, where, why. You as the reader need to understand—**who** wrote the book? **What,** in summation, is the book saying? **Why** was the book written? **When** was the book written? **Where** does the book intend to go or take me? Find out for yourself. **Faith, Obedience** and **Sacrifice** {**as inspired by the Holy Spirit**} is an individual experience everyone 'wills' to have with God. Don't you want yours to be a positive one? Everyone's experience is different. Get to know Him for yourself. Meditate on His sovereignty and on the paths your life has taken you. Through your periods of joy, sorrow, and revelation: Trust Him. God will bring unexpected blessings. The more you meditate on Him, the more He will lead you deeper and deeper into His word in hope that you will start to live by His word, thus obeying His word. You will reap wonderful benefits by being a doer (James 1:21-25). Being a doer means **obeying** His word.

Don't you want a joyful, spirit filled, intimate life with Christ?

Ignorance Is not Bliss - You Make the Call/It's Your Decision

Philosophers and scholars all over the world have ideas regarding religions that have greatly influenced millions of people. These religions have ruled out the concept of God the Trinity. The average followers of these so-called religions have become preoccupied with the worship of relics and idols, gods and demons, ancestors and spirits, inclusive of performing rituals, mantras, and various other practices. The fundamental concept of a Supreme Being by whose will everything exists and operates has been ignored and is constantly being ignored.

The various forms of meditations, fasting, yoga, and extreme self-denial will not bring you spiritual peace or enlightenment solely on the merit of self or self-idolship.

The God I serve is the only true God. The Bible in its many languages and several available versions, inspired and author by the Holy Spirit, is not hard to understand, although we say and think that it is. What seems hard is that it is hard to believe and even harder to obey its contents. BAMM! HELLO! That's why Jesus the Christ came. He came to fulfill the Scripture, that through Him you may be saved. Everything reverts back to the Scripture. From Buddha to Mohammed. From astrometry to astrology. It's all in the Manual. ONE GOD, ONE FAITH, ONE BAPTISM. THE FATHER, THE SON, THE HOLY SPIRIT. THE UNKNOWN GOD IS GOD OF ALL. THE UNKNOWN GOD is THE LION OF THE TRIBE OF JUDAH. THE UNKNOWN GOD is THE ROOT OF DAVID (Rev.5:5). THE UNKNOWN GOD is THE ALPHA and OMEGA, THE FIRST and LAST (Rev.1:8). This UNKNOWN GOD is THE LORD GOD who rules over all. He was, He is, and He is to come (Rev.4:8b). He is worthy to receive glory and honor and power. He is worthy because He created all things (Rev. 4:11).

Thinking that ignorance is bliss will cause Him to "spit you out of His mouth," (Rev.3:16). Salvation belongs to God who sits on the throne. Salvation also belongs to the Lamb (Rev.7:10). Ignorance is causing you to lose respect for the Maker and Creator of all things; you better recognize! You better act like you know! The God of Abraham, Isaac, and Jacob is our GOD. No, ignorance is not bliss. Choose ye this day who you will serve: Satan the accuser who brings charges against our brothers and sisters before God both day and night, or GOD THE ALMIGHTY who has defeated Satan. Satan has been defeated by the blood of the LAMB. He roams the earth seeking who and whom he can prey on. He is very angry. He knows his time is short (Rev.12:12). He makes war with God's children. We, who obey God's commands, hold firmly to what Jesus has said (Rev.12:17). Satan believes he has authority over every tribe, people, language, and nation. He has told lies about God's character and about the place where God lives and about those who live in Heaven with Him (Rev.13:6).

We, the people of God, must remain patient and faithful. We must remain faithful to Jesus. Faithful and obedient. Those who have died in the Lord are resting from their labor. The Holy Spirit states "What they have done will not be forgotten." Your ignorance will cause you to experience God's anger. The last days are upon us. Plagues will come to complete God's anger (Rev.15:1). Don't refuse to turn from your sins. Be mindful to give God glory. His judgment will be true and fair. Praise God all you who have respect for Him both great and small. The Greatest King of all and the most powerful Lord of all.

BLESSED BE THE NAME OF THE LORD.

The Importance of the Blood

There is power in the blood, the word, and the name of Jesus. Blood is atonement for your forefather's sins and atonement for our sins.

In the day of our forefathers, the blood of lambs, goats, bulls, birds, etc. had to be literally sacrificed on our behalf. In Exodus Chapter 12, the blood of a flawless male lamb was commanded by God to be literally applied (sacrificed) to each door post. This is called the Passover in which death passed over each Israelite's house. This was the final plague brought against the Egyptians' first-born sons. God mercifully spared the Israelites' first-born sons. The sacrificial offering of blood contains everything for the atonement of sins. We were—and are—a stiff necked people that blood sacrifices became overwhelming. We are of such a sin sick nature that we constantly stirred up God's wrath and anger against us. But instead of God wiping us off the face of the earth because of our sins, His infinite love for us would not allow Him.

He did away with the numerous amounts of blood sacrifices. He sent His son, the Lamb of God, Who gave His life for all of us once and for all (Rev.12:11). For, without the shedding of blood, there is no remission of sins. Satan, who brings charges against our brothers and sisters and present accusations before our God day and night, has been overcome because of the blood. Satan, you ain't got nothing on me. That lunatic has come down to the earth and sea. He is very angry because he knows his time is short. So beware. Wear the entire armor of God everyday less the adversary slip in. He is constantly seeking anyone he can devour.

However, eternal death has been swallowed up in the blood. Jesus has all authority because of the blood He shed for all of us on Calvary. Put your **faith** in the blood of Christ, which is life. Thank God for Christ's **obedience** to the cross. The Lord has taken away the authority of evil people. He has broken the power of rulers. When they (the rulers) became angry, they struck nations down. Their blows never stopped (Isaiah 14:5). However, the Lord who rules over all has said, "You can be sure that what I have planned will happen. What I have decided will take place. On my mountains I will walk all over them. The yokes they put on my people will be removed. The heavy load they put on their shoulders will be taken away." The Lord will reach out His powerful Hand. Who can keep Him from using it (Isaiah 14:24-27)?

Rely on the blood of Christ. It contains the measure of God's love for us. For we were brought with a price. Christ carried our sins in his body to the cross. He did it so that we would die, as far as sins are concerned, in hopes that we would lead godly lives. His wounds have made us whole. We are like sheep who have wondered away. His blood by **faith** has given us a way back to the Shepherd. He is the Leader of our souls (1Peter2:24-25). We belong to God. For, with the blood, He purchased our redemption. No, not the blood of goats and calves, but by spilling His own blood. He paid the price to set us free from sin forever. Christ offered Himself to God without any flaw. He did this through the power of the eternal Holy Spirit. So how much more will His blood wash from our minds our feelings of guilt for committing sin! Sin always leads to death. But now we can serve the living God. Christ is the propitiation for our sins. He is the go between of a new covenant. He died to set men free from the sins they committed under the first covenant (Heb.9:11-15).

As water cleanses our skin, the blood cleanses our soul. With the blood, something has to die in order for something to live, as done in sacrificial offerings. This time, Christ did it once and for all. Being washed in the blood will cause the seed of forgiveness to be planted in your heart, followed by the seed of charity (love), tithing, and the rest of the seeds of the fruit of the spirit. This brings on repentance and confession. Repentance is what sinners do before they become saints. Repentance is a reversal (change of mind) to trust (from yourself to God). Confession is what saints do when they sin. Confession is agreement (identity) with the sin against God. Read Psalms 51. Ask God to restore unto you 'the joy of thy salvation' (Psalm 51:12). For Jesus did not come to call the righteous but sinners unto repentance (Mark 2:17). It's better to repent in sorrow today than confess in terror at the judgment (4/7/08 *Confession, Days of Praise*—2008 Inst. For Creation Research 2008).

God has found everyone guilty of not obeying Him. Through Christ the Lord, God can have mercy on you. Go to God in the name of Jesus and await your miracle. The wind cometh and goeth. You can't see it. But you know it has been there. Plant your faith seed in your heart and obey. You will feel the manifestation of Jesus Christ within you. I know.

Peter's Faith

Simon Peter, one of Christ's beloved disciples, loved Jesus very much. Jesus called him into discipleship when Andrew (Simon's brother) introduced them. Jesus looked at Simon and said "You will be called Cephas" (which, when translated, means Peter) John 1: 41-42. Simon Peter became a devoted follower. However, as it got close to Jesus's arrest, Peter said to Jesus "I will lay down my life for you," (John 13:37). Jesus answered, "Will you really lay down your life for me? SIMON, SIMON, Satan has asked to sift you as wheat. But I have prayed for you, Simon that your faith may not fail. And when you have turned back, strengthen your brother," (Luke 22: 31-32. I tell you the truth, before the rooster crows, you will disown me three times, (John 13:38.

Although we are to bear our own load, we are too bearing one another's burdens. No one is better than one's neighbor. We are to help each other. Jesus did not pray that Simon Peter would not deny Him; He prayed that his faith would not fail him. Know why? I'll tell you why. When Peter denied Christ the third time, the rooster crowed. The Lord turned and looked straight at Peter. Peter remembered the Lord's words in reference to his denial. He then went outside and wept bitterly (Luke 22:62). At that very moment, Satan could have started to have a field day with Peter in several ways. One, by causing Peter to feel very guilty about denying Christ. Peter also lied about denying the Christ, and this was also brought to remembrance. Peter was loyal to Jesus but when he turned his back on Him and betrayed Him, I'm sure he [Peter] felt like nothing. He felt unhappy and miserable. He was perhaps wishing something would happen to take it (the pain) away. When Peter wept, he felt soooo empty inside, full of remorse. Something did happen, because Jesus had prayed Peter knew that although he denied knowing Him, Jesus did not and would not abandon him. Why? Because Jesus prayed that Peter's faith would not fail him. Because of Peter's faith, Peter knew he could go back to Jesus to ask for forgiveness. Because of Peter's faith, he knew Jesus still loved him unconditionally. If Jesus did not pray the prayer He prayed, it would have been a possibility that Satan would have tried to capitalize on the guilt Peter felt. Remember, Satan asked permission to sift Peter as wheat. But with Jesus praying for Peter's faith, Peter was safe and secure in the arms of Jesus' love. Thus, Peter continued his discipleship in the faith to mission, evangelize, and do miracles by the power of the Holy Ghost in Jesus' name.

The pain that Peter felt when he denied Jesus cannot and did not compare to the horrible intense pain that our beloved Christ felt knowing He was about to take the sins of the world to the cross. Peter and the rest of us guilty sinners would be declared righteous by Jesus paying our penalty. We are not saved by our righteousness, but by His mercy. As it is written: By grace are we saved through faith; and not of ourselves, for it is the gift of God. Not how good we have been, so no man can boast. For apart from the cross, we are lost. Our Savior had to shed blood on our behalf or there would have been no forgiveness. The cross is not a symbol of religion; it is the greatest of all gifts. For apart from the cross, we rebelled against Him, denied Him, lied to Him, betrayed Him, and walked out of God's will. But because we have accepted the death of His Son as full payment for our sins, He sits on the right hand side of the Father and declares us no longer guilty.

As Peter denied Jesus three times, Jesus asked Peter three times "Do you love me, Peter?" That was Peter's reinstatement. Jesus let Peter know that through his faith in Jesus, he [Peter] had the victory (John 21:17). So in essence, sons and daughters of God, when you do something wrong, don't beat yourself up about it. Take it to the Lord in prayer. Use your faith and talk to the Lord. Repent and ask for forgiveness. Do not let guilt consume you, lest you fall victim to the adversary. For all have sinned and come short of the glory of God. None is perfect. No, not one.

Through faith, keep guilt from taking root in your heat. If it festers, it will give and make room for seeds of resentment, bitterness, and other negativeness. You do not want Satan to take advantage of this. Do not be ignorant of his devices (2Corint 2:11). Be forever mindful that Christ went to the cross to reconcile a sinful human race to Himself (Rom.5:10-11). Live by faith...not by your own feelings. When you let faith take the lead in your life, courage will follow. Come out of your comfort zone and practice your faith in serving God. His comfort zone is much more satisfying and comforting. I know this for I am a witness. Faith will keep you in His will. Staying in His Will will keep you obedient regarding His precepts. I am telling you from firsthand experience. Taste and see that the Lord is good (Psalms 34:8). For blessed are you who take refuge in Him. I once was young and now I am a little older. I have never seen the righteous forsaken nor His seed begging for bread (Psalm 34:25). So, delight yourself in the Lord and He will give you the desires of your heart (Psalm 37:4). When you are faithful over a few things, He will make you ruler over many things (Matt.25:21). Therefore, rejoice evermore. Pray without creasing. And, by golly, remember: in everything give thanks: for this is the will of God in Christ Jesus concerning you (Thessalonians 5: 16-18).

Staying in His will gives Him control over every detail in our lives. He is not off on more important business. He loves us dearly, and He is working out every aspect for good for us who love Him. Satan cannot touch us unless he first gets God's permission. Think back: Not only did He ask God's permission to sift Peter as wheat, but God also allowed Satan to test Job—not only once, but twice (See Job 1:8 and Job 2:3).

The only time God gives Satan permission is when God sees the wonderful potential within us, which is our great faith in Him. Satan seeks to destroy our joy. But as the song says...the world didn't give it and the world can't take it away. Our life is not in Satan's hands. Our life is in the Lord's hands and we can trust and thank Him in all circumstances. Try Him. Put your faith and trust in Him and you will see the manifestation of the Holy Spirit working out every detail of your very being. Ask and you will receive, that your joy may be complete (John 16:24). Stay within His will and become a part of His perfect plan to bring each of us into communion and fellowship with the Trinity. He loves us and this is one reason why He allows certain incidents and circumstances to bring our wrong "attitudes" to our attention. Don't be afraid that you have messed up your life so bad (as I did once) that you could be of no good use to anyone. Continue to thank God through prayer and praise. This is an act of obedience which will release power—Holy Ghost power into our lives. Thank God for every detail of your life. For He has permitted all of these things to happen in order to bring you to the place you are now. Those who make it through the difficult times reach a new plateau and realize that their used-to-be normal life cannot be prepared to the life He has for you in His will. The joy of the Lord is your strength (Nehemiah 8:10). Yolanda Adams once sang: "For the battle is not yours; it's the Lord's (2Chronicles 20:15). The Lord will carefully watch over you.

For if you have made Jesus Christ the Lord of your life, you have already taken the first step in applying your faith. Obedience will follow. The love of God has been born within you. Faith without works is dead (James 2:17). Faith works by love. For God is love (1John 4:16). A love for Christ and a love for our fellowman. I mean, in reality, our lives are not our own. No matter how much you think it is. You think you have control over your life to the point that you can stop someone from spying on you; think again. No matter how much you try to escape nosy persons, it just isn't going to happen. I know it makes you uncomfortable to think others know your deepest thoughts and darkest secrets. But the truth of the matter is: There is no place, and I do mean no place you and your girlfriend(s), boyfriend(s), lover(s), husband(s), wife (wives), friend(s), enemy (enemies), babies daddy (daddies), papa(s), maybe(s), etc., can go to hide from the Lord. Not only does He know what you did, who you did it to, how you did it, and when you did it, He knows everything about you. Neither you nor I can lie to God and get away with it; nor can we think we can rationalize with God to convince Him to buy our brand of logic. Check out Psalms 139. I did not say it.... It's in the Manual.

Also, check out the Proverbs: For it is a wise person who fear God, who cooperate to the best of his ability in Faith with God instead of resisting Him. I'm a witness. Every natural occurrence has an equal spiritual phenomenon. The longer a person fights an overwhelming force to do God's will, the more that person will get beat up. My arms and your arms are too short to box with God. Jonah tried to fight against doing God's will, but got swallowed up in the belly of a fish for three days and nights(Jonah 1:17). You will do God's will, especially if you have been ordained and predestined. Jacob wrestled with God all night, insisting on a blessing. He came away with a dislocated hip. He received his blessing, not because he was a great wrestler but because God had already ordained that he would be blessed (Genesis 32:25). I am telling you if we continue to resist God's calling, His tactics will become more forceful. Believe me, He can pursue longer than I have the strength to resist. I will become weaker and weaker. God knows me and He knows you. He will have His way. After all, we were brought with a price (the blood of His Son). In addition, we are not to think of ourselves more highly than we ought, but rather think of ourselves with sober judgment in accordance with the measure of faith God has given each of us (Romans 12:3). I've learned that if I patiently endure painful circumstances (and I have), and believe God is working for my good, my faith gradually and steadily increased. What about your faith? Have you noticed what Satan meant for bad turns out for good? Stay and walk in God's will and watch how the Holy Spirit works on your behalf. Use your faith and obey His word.

There is a serious spiritual warfare going on. If you stay in the word, it will change your life (Romans 13:14). I mean, it takes a mustard seed six to eight years to grow to its full potential. It does not reach maturity overnight, or in a year. Faith grows the same way—gradually. Everyone has been given a measure of faith. Growth is the nature of a seed. Nurture your faith with the consistency of obeying the word. You will see the manifestation. Keep believing and you will experience new spiritual strength as your faith increase. But if you do not nourish your faith, it will remain the size of a mustard seed and you will become discouraged. Daily nourishment of your faith will produce results. This is the victory that has overcome the world—our faith (1John 5:4). For everyone born of God overcomes the world. God can and will permit things to happen in our lives, things that have the potential to cause our faith to die. It happened to me in December 2007. Not only in December 2007, but the entire year of 2007. I was faced with opposition from beginning to end. Everywhere I turned, my faith was challenged—from January through November. I remember breaking down at my friends' abode. It seemed as if nobody wanted me. I could not get a job. Eventhough all the time I knew I had skills. I almost started to believe God didn't want me either. My faith was starting to fail me. I had been a trooper/warrior all of 2007. But I had reached my breaking point. The reality of it was I just did not want to face the truth of the matter. In December, it just got worse. Then, bamm! It dawn on me what was really going on. Keep reading, I'll tell you.

Satan was sifting me as wheat. But by God's grace, I was persevering. As Donnie McClure said "When you done all you can...stand." There's also a cliché that goes: "He who feels it...knows it." Believe me, if Vanessa is going to write a book about faith, obedience, and sacrifice, I had to go through it. Then it became clear just how intimately God is involved in our lives. He causes us to be where we need to be so that we can learn what we need to learn. When we see God for who He is, our faith grows. God is sovereign. We need to fear God. He is greater than our ability to understand Him. We simply cannot comprehend the whys and hows of His mysterious ways. All of us have a task: to trust and obey Him. We trust Him through faith. Without faith, it is impossible to please God (Heb. 11:6). Just trust God. He can cause our problems to work for us. He can turn them around. We can face the enemy. The Lord can make them work for our good. You began to see the picture much more clearly. I now know to trust that God is giving me the joy of seeing Him accomplish many good things in me. Joy is a dynamo that can cause my faith and your faith to work. At the beginning of 2008, I know God had intervened in my affairs. I had to trust Him. I did not know what I was up against, but I somehow had the comforting feeling that everything was going to be okay. I still had some small fears and I also realized that I had no one to lean on but Jesus. I had to stretch out on faith. God made it so that I had to depend on Him. He became my all in all.

There is a cliché' that says: FEAR is False Evidence Appearing Real. Also, once you know the facts, fear dissipates. Well, the facts were starting to unfold for me. But that's another story. I just know I really had to step out on faith now. I had no energy for fear or anxiety. I was obligated to trust and put my faith in God. I found out when you use your faith, you do not rely on what you see or feel. Feelings should not control faith. Faith should control feelings. Faith requires discipline. Don't be manipulated. If your faith in God declines, you will begin to dwell on your fears. Doubts start to set in. Then you start to think that God is not actively involved in your life and that you are not good enough for God to intervene in your life (I'm a witness). My life had become so messed up...that I thought God didn't even want me. You get caught up in situations to the point where it seems people and circumstances try to control who you are and where you end up. But the truth is they cannot control your reactions. Only you can do that. People try to upset you and make you angry. They think they can push your buttons. They want to see you react. Let it go! Let God. Don't react...respond. As long as your faith is in God's control, you are not defeated. With God, all things are possible. You can do no good thing without God's help and the aid of the Holy Spirit. Sometimes, it seems as if your life gets to the point that you have nothing working for you. You are still one of God's most treasured children. Now, let's keep it real. Check the Manual. You will notice that every other person in the Bible had severe problems. These were the people God used. You are no exception. Don't let your faith fail. Keep building, for when the unexpected happens, let your faith take over so that fears will not control your thoughts. Let persistence kick in.

Continue to trust God, and watch Him reward you with great joy, happiness, and inner strength. This requires commitment. Try it. It's better than living according to the world. Often, we are afraid to trust Him because we think He wants to make life difficult. He knows how much He could help us, but He wants us to want His presence. God loves us very much and wants to communicate with us. But we prefer not to have fellowship with Him. He will not force Himself on us. Peace of mind is based on faith that God is in control of our situation.

You and I will remain children of God, and we may think that we are living a Christian life. However, we will not be privy to His promised blessings until we learn to **obey** Him. Like it or not, that's the way it is. Obedience, is better than sacrifice (Matthew 5:23-24).

Now let's talk a little about obedience....

Obedience-Related Bible Verses

1st Samuel 15:22
    Deut 6:3
    John 14:23
    Acts 5:29-32
    Matthew 5:23
    Matthew 6:33
    Psalms 7:15-17

1st John 2:1-6—Do you know Him? My little children, these things I write to you, so that you may not sin. And if anyone sins, we have an advocate with the Father, Jesus Christ, the righteous. He Himself is the propitiation for our sins, and not for ours only but also for the whole world. Now by this we know that we know Him, if we keep His commandments. He who says, "I know Him," and does not keep His commandments, is a liar, and the truth is not in him. But whoever keeps His word, truly the love of God is perfected in him. By this we know that we are in Him. He who says he abides in Him ought himself also to walk just as He walked.

    Psalms 84:11
    Psalms 119:2
    Psalms 119:5-7
    Psalms 19: 9-11
    Joshua 1:8

Samson's Disobedience

Samson being a Nazarite was set apart to God since birth. He was instructed never to cut his hair or his strength would leave him and he would become as weak as any other man. Delilah nagged him into telling her how he kept his strength. Once she found out, she wooed him to sleep in her lap and had his head shaven. The spirit of the Lord left Samson once his hair was gone.

The Philistines seized him, gouged out his eyes, and put him in shackles in prison. The Philistines then used Samson as a puppet on a string. Samson prayed to the Lord to remember him and give him strength once more to defeat the Philistines for taking his two eyes. The Lord gave Samson his strength back and he killed more Philistines at that time than when he was living (Judges 16).

Jonah's Disobedience
Then there was Jonah who tried to flee from the Lord and ended up in the belly of a fish for three days. From the belly of the fish, Jonah prayed to the Lord and the Lord delivered Jonah out of the belly of the fish. The Lord commanded Jonah a second time, "Go to the great city of Nineveh and proclaim to it the message of the Lord," (Jonah 3:2). Jonah obeyed the word of the Lord and went to Nineveh. When God saw what they did and how they turned from their evil ways, He had compassion and did not bring upon them the destruction He had threatened.

Obedience to God's Word
Malachi chapter three states that the Lord changes not. That ever since the days of Abraham, Isaac, and Jacob, we have not kept His ordinances. "Return to me and I will return to you." How? By obeying His word. Giving back to God just a portion of what He continually gives us. Give back by making sure there is food in His storehouse. Give in tithes and offerings. Try Him now and "See if I will not throw open the floodgates of heaven and pour out so much blessing that you will not have room enough for it," (Malachi 3:10).

Ten Healed of Leprosy (Luke 17:11-17)
Ten men who had leprosy met Jesus as He was traveling between Samaria and Galilee. They asked Him to have pity on them. Jesus told them to go and "Show yourselves to the priests." As they went (obeying the word of the Lord), they were cleansed. Only one (a foreigner) came back to thank Jesus, although there were ten. Because of his faith and obedience, and him rendering the sacrifice of praise, he was made whole. Which means not only was he healed from his leprosy, he was restored as if he was never sick. Praise God.

Jesus' Burial
When Jesus died, a man named Joseph took Jesus' body down from the cross, wrapped it in linen cloth, and placed Him in a tomb. The Sabbath was about to begin. The women, who had followed Jesus to the cross, followed Joseph and saw the tomb. They acknowledged how the body was laid in it. They then went home to prepare spices and perfumes for Jesus' body. But they were mindful to rest on the Sabbath. They did this in obedience to God's commandment.

The proof of our love for God is our obedience to the commandments of God.

Obedient to the Faith

Do what thus said the Lord and you will live a peaceful and contented life. Be obedient to the faith. Psalm 37:25 says, "I once was young, but now I am old and I have never seen the righteous forsaken, nor his descendants begging bread." The word is true. What child of God who have kept the faith, and obeyed the Lord has been seen begging? Not one. Amen. God is faithful to His promises.

Do you know how many blessings we have lost or forfeited by being disobedient? How many of our lives have gone astray by being disobedient? If it has not been for His love, mercy, grace, and compassion, I tremble to think where we would be. Even in our disobedience, God continues to rescue us from our troubles. But oh...how long? Do you fear God?

Obedience

Jesus' obedience to God provided our salvation. Our obedience makes us workers with Him. Our Bible tells us in Matthew 6:33, "Seek first His Kingdom and His righteousness and all these things will be given to you as well...." This verse covers us when it comes to being obedient. If we seek first His kingdom, we will do what thus said the Lord. We will follow His commandments. If thou love the Lord thy God with all thy heart and all our soul, and with our entire mind, we will obey His will. Everything hangs on this commandment and the commandment that we love our neighbor as ourselves. You will try to do what is right all the time. No one is perfect, but obedience is better than sacrifice. Your sacrifice is unacceptable if you have something against your brother. You have to right the wrong first, and then render to God your sacrifice. For just as I am writing this to you I am a witness if you do not settle matters quickly, adverse things will happen. It is written, once you reconcile with your brother, you can offer your gift at the altar and all will be made well. If you owe a debt to society (such as the courts), pay it. Or they will hand you over to the officer who will throw you into jail (prison) (Matthew 5: 25-26). Be obedient in the beginning and jail may not be a part of your ending. In being disobedient, you eventually get caught. Sometimes, we get this false illusion that we are capable of doing our own thing and get away with it. A lot of us are rebels at heart, but we must learn how to get along with other people—Our friends, neighbors, co-workers, and superiors. Being obedient to the Lord enables you to do just that and even more. Being **obedient** means going out on a limb and trusting God without anything to hold on to but **faith**. Get to know Him. Read His Word. The more you read His Word, the more you will believe in Him. Then you would want to be obedient to the impressions and urgings from the Holy Spirit within yourself. Thus, faith believes in something you don't see, but you sure will feel Him and His presence working good for you. Wouldn't you rather be obedient to God and see His power demonstrated in and concerning your life, than be seeking the temporal approval of man? The substance of man is of a shallow nature, being obedient to God sometimes means going against the expressed wishes of the people who came or may come to ask for help. I experienced this in my own home. My son moved in with me after living several years with his father simply because his father would not let him have his way. I truly wished I would not have given in so easy. He brought with him an entourage of friends which turned out to be the demons from hell. Believe me if I would have taken the issue to the Throne of grace I assure you they would have never crossed the front porch. On this issue, I should have listened to my ex-husband. But being a mother, I listened to my son. I was just too easy on him. Needless to say, his friends didn't leave until hell almost froze over. By that time, the quality of my life dwindled. My obedience to the Lord went out the window. To say the least, my life became very unmanageable trying to deal with life's ups and downs by myself. I started letting my fears control me and the direction life was taking me. Although I still trusted God, I obviously did not trust Him enough to turn my life back over to Him and be obedient. The fears I felt started dominating my behavior. I had lost my courage and became a slave to my fears and the ruler of this weak sinful world. I had forgotten that in Christ, I had been given authority over my fears. My reluctance to admit my fears caused me to deny them. When I did face them, I tried to fight and control them. In doing so, it controlled me to the point almost of paralysis. I had to remember God had not given us a spirit of fear, but of a sound mind. I possess a lot of energy and I was not about to let my fears and anxieties suck it up. My priorities were out of balance. I was definitely in spiritual jeopardy. I was putting the wrong things first. As with everything, I was in the process of dying. Every plant and animal (and most humans) struggle to stay alive. Appearances can be deceptive. I was smiling on the outside, but dying on the inside. I needed to get back on the right track. But how? I needed to talk to someone who to me was representation of God. Putting my faith in God helped me defeat and destroy fear. The only fear I wanted to feel was the fear of God. To do His will. For not to do His will was to suffer greatly. In Christ, I had already won the spiritual battle with fear. In Revelations 2:4 the Lord states: "I have this against you, that you have left your first love." I had become the prodigal daughter and strayed from God. I had to find my way back home. Being a Christian, I had berated myself unmercifully for failing to obey Christ. I started to become tongue-tied when the opportunity presented itself to testify and share Christ with unbelievers. I allowed myself to be divided. Matthew 12:25 states, "a house divided against itself cannot stand." I had picked up a lack of confidence in myself and in God. Things were not going the way I wanted them to go. It was in going through these trying times (trials and tribulations) that God was carrying me.

The power of Christ rested in His decision to follow and do God's will. Once, His mother and stepfather were looking for Him. After three days, they found Him in the temple courts. He was in His Father's house about His

Father's business, (Luke 2:41-50. His obedience to God provided our salvation and His obedience to His mother caused her to treasure their days together in her heart (Luke 2:51-52). Our obedience to Him shows our love for Him and we will learn and obey His teachings (John 14:23, 24). Obeying Him causes us to be a part of Him. As long as we remain in Him and He in us, we will bear much fruit. This is in spite of the economic crisis going on. If we put our stock in the economy and not in the Lord, we will come up empty handed. For, apart from God, we can do nothing (Luke 15:5). Luke 15:7 says, "If you remain in me and my words remain in you, ask whatever you wish, and it will be given you," (Luke 15:10). "If you obey my commands, you will remain in my love, just as I have obeyed my Father's commands and remain in His love." We are children of God, but we will not receive many of His promised blessings until we learn to obey Him. Like it or not, this is the will of God. God is in charge of everything. Be mindful to always give thanks (Eph. 5:20). So be careful to heed the warning from Israel's history. Don't look upon someone and say "Oh, I would never be like that or that could never happen to me. Or I don't know why they can't pick their selves up." You, too, could fall into sin, for it is only by God's grace you have not. Watch and pray. Don't murmur against God and His dealings with you. A particular sin (sickness or disease) can lie undetected as it works its destruction. 1Corinthians 10 tells us to be careful. Stay obedient. Do not test the Lord. If you think you are standing firm, be careful that you don't succumb to temptation, 1Corinthians 10:12. I am a living witness. There will always be people around us who need improvement. We all have our own issues and problems. However, God will take a problem and make it work for our good. He will use His awesome power to reward our trust in Him. He can take an evil scheme that Satan devised and make it work for our good. Life's bitter and painful experiences are used by God for our good to produce His peace in us, in which we will experience incredible joy. We did not choose Him. He chose and appointed us to go and bear fruit (John 15:16, 17). Just obey His command: Love each other.

A Key Factor

Obedience has been a key factor since the beginning of time. Adam and Eve disobeyed God in the Garden of Eden, causing sin to enter in the world. Sin became so great in man's heart that the Lord regretted that He had made man (See Gen 6:5). Thank God for the obedience and faithfulness of Noah. Noah obeyed God, thus preserving life, for God wiped out every living thing except for Noah's family and two of every living creature on earth through the flood (See Gen 6 and 7).

The people of Sodom and Gomorrah were wiped out because of their wickedness and disobedience. Only one family was found worthy. That was the family of Lot. Lot, his sons, and wife escaped God's wrath because he obeyed the Lord's command to leave the city. The Lord's angels guided them out of the city by God's mercy. As soon as they reached their destination, the Lord rained down burning sulfur on Sodom and Gomorrah out of the heavens. Lot's wife looked backed and she became a pillar of salt (disobedience, Genesis 19).

Abraham obeyed the Lord when he was tested to give his only son Isaac as a burnt offering (Gen 22). Because of his obedience and his fear of the Lord, the Lord acknowledged Abraham's faith by blessing him and making his descendants as numerous as the stars in the sky and as the sand on the seashore. God advised him "that through his offspring all nations on earth will be blessed because you have obeyed me," (Gen 22:18).

The Lord advised Joshua to "be strong and very courageous. Be careful to obey all the law my servant Moses gave you; do not turn from it to the right or to the left, that you may be successful wherever you go." "Do not let this Book of the Law (See section on Bible Overview) (The history books—first five books of the Bible) depart from your mouth; meditate on it day and night, so that you may be careful to do everything written in it. Then you will be prosperous and successful," (Joshua 1:7-8).

Because the prostitute Rahab feared the Lord, she hid the spies Joshua sent to "check out" Jericho. Because of this, she asked that her family be spared when Joshua and his army invaded Jericho. Joshua's spies obeyed Rahab's instruction when they departed from her house, which was on the wall of the city (Joshua 2), thus causing Rahab's family to be spared when the walls came tumbling down.

Which Comes First: Obedience or Sacrifice?
In 1 Samuel 15, Saul did not follow the Lord's instruction. The Lord instructed him to destroy everything. But Saul did not destroy everything. He spared the best of the sheep, the best of the cattle, the best of the calves, and the best of the lambs. Everything else they (he and his army) destroyed. The Lord was grieved that He had made Saul king. The word went to Samuel that Saul had not carried out the Lord's instructions and Samuel was troubled. Saul told Samuel that he did in fact carry out the Lord's instruction. Well, Samuel said, "If this is so, how come I hear sheep and cattle in the background?" Saul said, "Oh, we kept the best to sacrifice to the Lord." Samuel said, "Wait a minute. The Lord sent you on a mission to completely destroy those wicked people" and "destroy everything that belongs to them." Saul responded by saying, "I went on the mission the Lord assigned me," but brought back the King (Agag) and the best of the cattle and sheep to sacrifice them to the Lord your God." But Samuel replied: "Does the Lord delight in burnt offerings and sacrifices as much as in obeying the voice of the Lord? To obey is better than sacrifice, and to heed is better than the fat of rams." Then Saul acknowledged that he violated the Lord's command and instruction. Saul eventually took his own life. What a tragic ending.

Sacrifice-Related Bible Verses

Ezekiel 36:26
2 Corinthians 5:17
Revelations 21:5
Philippians 1:6
Isaiah 49:13
Isaiah 63:9
Revelation 2:10
Genesis 18:14
Psalms 37:24
Micah 7:7
Colossians 3:15-17
John 3:16

The Ultimate Sacrifice

The greatest sacrifice was made by God "who so loved the world gave His son, that whosoever believes in Him shall not perish but have eternal life," (John 3:16). The ultimate sacrifice made by our Lord and Savior Jesus Christ was for the remission of our sins. We are such a stiff-necked people. Because of our disobedience to God's precepts, which consists of His Ten Commandments and over 600 laws for our daily conduct, we were constantly rendering blood sacrifices. We were bringing Him meaningless offerings. This has caused God to deal harshly with us. The prophets warned us of His impending punishments for our idolatrous worship. We sinned so greatly that the Lord had to send judges, kings, and a series of prophets to judge and deal with us according to our wrongdoings and to guide us back to Jehovah. The prophets were continually praying for us and bringing us God's message. They had great leadership skills. We were constantly burdening them with our issues, which we created because of our constant and continuous disobedience. The Bible has about eighteen books that bear prophet names.

We are still doing the same today, burdening our spiritual leaders with our issues. The majority of these issues are related to our disobedience to the ways of God. If we would just obey His will, our lives would be much more manageable.

But our disobedience brought pain, suffering, lying, cheating, and all kinds of wickedness. Each generation became more and more perverse. We became strangers to God's way and to His commandments. We drifted further and further away from our Father. We became a people with no hope. No direction and no purpose. We needed an ultimate blood sacrifice. We needed the Lamb of God, for we are as filthy rags. We needed to be washed and cleansed, and because of God's agape love for us, He sent His son, His only begotten Son to deliver us from the power of darkness.

We are His creation. Along life's journey we got to thinking that we were gods ourselves. Instead of worshipping the Father almighty, we started worshipping each other, along with tangible things. We became very vain to the point we started calling "shots" like we hold the world in our hands.

However, my brothers and sisters, let's remind ourselves that the earth is the Lord's, even the world, and we that dwell within. Everything belongs to God. Instead of God wiping us out with one sweep of His Hand, His love for us got the best of Him, and He sacrificed His Son to die on our behalf. A human sacrifice had to be made in order to make things right with God. So Jesus came down to carry our sins to the cross. He was perfect in every way and was without sin. When He died on that cross for us, our sins were so great in number and so ugly and distasteful God had to turn His back to Jesus while He hung up on the cross. Jesus said, "My God, My God, why have thou forsaken me?" It got dark and the sun refused to shine while my Lord hung up on the cross for you and me. Then Jesus commended His spirit into the hands of God and said, "It is finish." Jesus obeyed God on our behalf. He could have saved Himself, but He decided to die for your soul and mine. To God be the glory. Thank you, Jesus.

Well, it doesn't stop there. Weeping may endure for a night, but joy cometh in the morning. On the first day of the week, Jesus declared victory over death. He got up from the grave. He appeared to His disciples and others then ascended into the heavens where He now sits on the right hand side of the Father. There is no other name to save man but the name of Jesus. He is our Lord and Redeemer. Our sins have been taken care of by the sacrificial death of Christ our Lord. We now have redemption through His blood. Whosoever believes in Him should not perish but have everlasting life (John 3:15). In spite of all our sins and failures, we are justified by faith and have peace with God through our Lord Jesus Christ (Romans 5:1); that if any man sins, we have an advocate with the Father (1John 2:1). Jesus is the only mediator between us and the Father, for He is the propitiation for our sins, that if we obey His Word, God's love is made complete in us (1John 2:5).

God sacrificed His Son for us. Now, by His amazing grace, are we saved through faith and not by ourselves. This is a gift from God. Through faith, we are to be obedient to His Word. In being obedient, we will sacrifice our time, talent, and tithes. We will do so by exhibiting the fruit of the spirit. For our sacrifices mean absolutely nothing if we harbor hatred for each other and do not exhibit the fruit of the spirit. These are love, joy, peace, patience, kindness, goodness, faithfulness, gentleness, and self-control (Galatians 5:22, 23).

Let's keep it real—God is not mocked. Whatever a man soweth, that he shall reap. If he sows to please his sinful nature, from that nature will reap destruction. If he sows to please the spirit, from the spirit will reap eternal life (Galatians 6:7-8). Therefore, as we have an opportunity, let us do good to all people, especially to those who belong to the family of believers (Galatians 6:10).

The Lord had a chosen nation who rejected Him. But thanks be to the love of Christ who said "whosoever will let him come." The Lord had a chosen nation. He came to them and they received Him not. This was prophesied by the prophets in the old testament. Isaiah 65 states He had to reveal Himself to those who did not ask for Him. The Jews and other nations did not receive Him. God was there for them and they rejected Him. He said "Here am I, here am I!" He held out His Hands for them. But they continued to provoke Him to His face. We his people became stiff-necked evildoers.

Jesus came and said who-so-ever believes in Him is not condemned. That whosoever believes in Him shall not perish but have everlasting life. That whosoever wants, let him come. For Jesus is the stone that the builders rejected (Acts 4:11). His perfect life qualified Him to die in our place and pay our sin debt in full. We are here because of His sacrifice and love for us. We are still here because of the wonderful presence of the Holy Spirit, which continually make intercessions for us to the Father. Because of the sacrifice of Jesus, we have the gift of The Holy Spirit. It is the Holy Spirit who saves us from ourselves.

Seek God constantly. Establish an awesome relationship with Him, for He gives us life and free will. Be an example to someone. Let them see your joy in Christ Jesus. Acknowledge your sin before the Lord and He will forgive the guilt of your sin (Psalm 32). The truth shall set you free. Anything you hide has power and authority over you. Don't be afraid of what someone is going to think or say. Do you want to please God or man?

God is calling out to you, to us every day. Seek Him while He can be found. Do not reject Him. Stop ignoring His advice. Stop being so sometimey, only calling on Him when distressed and when trouble overwhelms you. He has preserved your life and my life. He has kept our feet from slipping (Psalm 66:9). Let's fulfill our vows to Him. Let's take our offerings to the temple. So many of us think, "Oh, if I give tithes to the church, the pastor will ride in a fine car and live in a finer house than mine's." So I will put my faith in man (myself), and obey my will, and put my offerings and sacrifices in tangible things the way I see fit. But woe, woe, woe....

Will a man rob God? Just who do we think we are? We have robbed Him by taking His money and doing wicked and deceitful things with it. Think about it. We won't even give back 10 percent of what He has given us. We barely give to one another unless it is benefiting us in one way or another. We have become a selfish and self-centered people. We have gotten to the point that we don't want to help no one out unless there is something in it for us (WIIFM). We have even gotten to the point that some of us don't even want to give (sacrifice) our time or talents back to God who made us. We have come to the point that we feel as though we only have time for our jobs and ourselves. We have put our trust and faith in our jobs, family, children, houses, cars, and the finite things of this world. We disobey authorities and cater to our own selfish wants. We have become a people of "I'll scratch your back if you scratch mine." I'll do you a favor if you do this for me. We are looking for a quick return on our so-called sacrifices. We don't have time to help anyone out unless a "fee" or "price", or exchange is involved. Something we can see.

Well…my brothers and sisters…. ATTENTION…. ATTENTION…ATTENTION…NEWSFLASH…STOP THE PRESS….

HEADLINER: Let me give you the HAND—

Psalm 24:1(NKJV) says The earth is the Lord's, and all its fullness, The world, and those who dwell therein.

Psalm 24:1(NIV) says The earth is the Lord's, and everything in it, the world, and all who live in it.

Psalm 24:1(NIRV) says The earth belongs to the Lord. And so does everything in it. The world belongs to Him. And so does all who live in it.

So as you see, who are you and who am I to determine when and what we give back to the Lord? He has already told us in His Instruction Manual how much to give. Blessed be the name of the Lord and thank God for Jesus. There are over 600 laws in addition to the ten commandments that we would have to adhere to if it had not been for the Lord sending Jesus to die on our behalf. What can I render to God for all His mercy? A 10 percent of our tithes plus offerings and a portion of our first fruit. Render this along with a broken spirit and a contrite and broken heart. For this God will not despise (Psalm 51:17). Render the sacrifices of praise. Render the sacrifices of thanksgiving. Be humble and share with each other the fruit of the spirit which are contained within one's heart (Gal 5:22-23). Be joyful in giving. Above all, walk in obedience to His commandments and walk in love (1John 1:16). Be thankful for all that is given to you. And be faithful to the one that gives to all.

For there is no one righteous, not even one; and there is no one who understands, no one who seeks God. All have turned away (Romans 3:10-12). So be thankful of our mediator and advocator, who is Christ Jesus.

Stop storing treasures here on earth where moth and rust destroy, and where thieves break in and steal. But store up for yourselves treasures in heaven (Matthew 6:19-20). For where your treasure is, there your heart will be also (Matthew 6:21).

Jesus—His Genealogy as the Son of Man (The Son of God)

John 19:2: The soldiers twisted together a crown of thorns and put it on his head.

Revelation 14:14: I looked, and there before me was a white cloud, and seated on the cloud was one "like a son of man" with a crown of gold on his head and a sharp sickle in his hand.

This is the last of the eighty-seven New Testament references (eighty-four in the four gospels, one in the Acts, none found in the Epistles, and two in the Revelation) to Jesus Christ as the Son of Man.

The Revelation states He came back the way He ascended into heaven after His Resurrection as King of all the Earth.

After John the Baptist baptized Jesus, He prayed and while He prayed, the heaven was opened. The Holy Spirit descended like a dove upon Him. God spoke from heaven saying, "You are my beloved Son, in you I am well pleased."

Jesus began His ministry at about thirty years of age, being(as was supposed) the son of Joseph, the son of Heli, the son of Matthat, the son of Levi, the son of Melchi, the son of Janna, the son of Joseph, the son of Mattathiah, the son of Amos, the son of Nahum, the son of Esli, the son of Naggai, the son of Maath, the son of Mattathiah, the son of Semei, the son of Joseph, the son of Judah, the son of Joannas, the son of Rhesa, the son of Zerubbabel, the son of Shealtiel, the son of Neri, the son of Melchi, the son of Addi, the son of Cosam, the son of Elmodam, the son of Er, the son of Jose, the son of Eliezer, the son of Jorim, the son of Matthat, the son of Levi, the son of Simeon, the son of Judah, the son of Joseph, the son of Jonan, the son of Eliakim, the son of Melea, the son of Menan, the son of Mattathah, the son of Nathan, the son of David, the son of Jesse, the son of Obed, the son of Boaz, the son of Salmon, the son of Nahshon, the son of Amminadab, the son of

Rani, the son of Hezron, the son of Perez, the son of Judah, the son of Jacob, the son of Isaac, the son of Abraham, the son of Terah, the son of Nahor, the son of Serug, the son of Reu, the son of Peleg, the son of Eber, the son of Shelah, the son of Cainan, the son of Arphaxad, the son of Shem, the son of Noah, the son of Lamech, the son of Methuselah, the son of Enoch, the son of Jared, the son of Mahalalel, the son of Cainan, the son of Enosh, the son of Seth, the son of Adam, the son of God.

The Causes of Our Problems

The Bible shows that Satan the Devil was the cause of Job's tragedies. (Job 1:7-12; 2:3-8). Furthermore, it identifies Satan as the chief source of our problems today when it states: "Woe for the earth and for the sea, because the Devil has come down to you, having great anger, knowing he has a short period of time," (Revelation 12:12). As "the ruler of this world," Satan has influenced many to engage in evil acts that have resulted in untold misery and heartache (John 12:31; Psalm 37:12, 14).

We should not, however, be quick to blame the Devil for every adversity we experience. As a result of inherited sin and imperfection, we are prone to make unwise decisions that can cause us problems (Psalm 51:5; Romans 5:12). For example, imagine a man who, by choice, neither eats properly nor gets sufficient rest. If this eventually leads to serious health problems, should he blame the Devil? No, the man has merely reaped the bitter consequences of his own poor judgment (Galatians 6:7). In such an instance, it is just as a Bible proverb puts it: "A man's own folly wrecks his life," (Proverbs 19:3, *The New English Bible*).

Finally, it must be realized that many unpleasant experiences are simply the result of "time and unforeseen occurrence," (Ecclesiastes 9:11). Consider the person who is unexpectedly caught in a rainstorm. Whether he will get a little wet or completely drenched may just depend on where he happens to be standing when the rain begins to fall. Similarly, in these "Critical hard times to deal with," negative conditions can quickly turn into a downpour of adversity (2 Timothy 3:1-5). To what extent we are personally affected is often a matter of timing and circumstances, over which we may have little or no control. Does this mean, then, that we will always be plagued with adversity?

Happily, Jehovah God will bring an end to all adversities very soon (Isaiah 25:8; Revelation 1:3; 21:3, 4). In the meantime, He shows that He really cares for us by providing "instruction" and "comfort from the Scriptures" so that we can cope with trials now as we look forward to that wonderful future just ahead (Romans 15:4; 1 Peter 5:7). At that time, those who are upright in God's eyes will enjoy unending life in a new world, free from every form of adversity (Psalm 37:29, 37).

Final Instructions

Encourage one another and build each other up, just as in fact you are commanded (1Thessalonians 4:11).

For God did not appoint us to suffer wrath but to receive salvation through our Lord Jesus Christ. He died for us so that, whether we are awake or sleep, we may live together with Him (1Thessalonians 4:9-10)

Now, may the Lord of Peace Himself give you peace at all times and in every way. (2Thessalonians 3:16a).

For in six days, the Lord made heaven and earth, and on the seventh day, He rested (Exodus 31:17 and Hebrews 4:4b). A day of rest and remembrance of Him as Creator and Savior.

If one of you should wander from the truth and someone should bring him back, remember this: Whoever turns a sinner from the error of his/her way, will save him/her from death and cover a multitude of sins (James 5:19).

The end of all things is near. Therefore, be clear-minded and self-controlled so that you can pray. Above all, love each other deeply, because love covers a multitude of sins (1Peter 4:7-8).

Last but not least: Grow in grace and knowledge of our Lord and Savior, Jesus Christ. To Him be the Glory both now and forever! Amen (2Peter 3:18).

To Him who is able to keep you from falling and to present you before His glorious presence without fault and with great joy—to the only God our Savior be glory, majesty, power and authority, through Jesus Christ our Lord, before all ages, now and forever more! Amen.

Lord I Pray to You

Psalm 69: 13-18 (NIRV)

May this be the time you show me your favor. God, answer me because you love me so much. Save me from the trouble I'm in. Save me from the deep water I'm in. Don't turn your face away from me. Answer me quickly. I'm in trouble. Come near and save me.

Everything Has Its Time
Book of Ecclesiastes 3:1-8

To everything there is a season,
A time for every purpose under heaven:
A time to be born,
And a time to die:
A time to plant,
And a time to pluck what is planted;
A time to kill,
And a time to heal;
A time to breakdown,
And a time to build up;
A time to weep,
And a time to laugh;
A time to mourn,
And a time to dance;
A time to cast away stones,
And a time to gather stones;
A time to embrace,
And a time to refrain from embracing;
A time to gain,
And a time to lose;
A time to keep,
And a time to throw away;
A time to tear,
And a time to sew;
A time to keep silence,
And a time to speak;
A time to love,

And a time to hate;
A time of war,
And a time of peace.

Forgiving One Another as God has forgiven You
Ephesians 4:32
Hit the Delete Button

Imagine living in a society where adulterers wear a scarlet letter and thieves wear a ball and chain. Imagine being identified only by your past. "They probably deserved it," you say. Really? Jesus said if you look at a member of the opposite sex with lust, you've committed adultery in your heart (Matt.5:28). Ouch! Then He went on to say that the standard of judgment you impose on others is the standard by which you'll be judged (Matt. 7:1-2). Can you live with that? Now, God's not soft on sin. His love won't let you off (Heb.12:6: Romans 8:38-39).

We're not too familiar with scarlet letters or balls and chains, but we are familiar with computers. And when someone hurts us or upsets us, God says "Forgive and hit the delete button!" Otherwise, you'll be corrupted with a virus that controls the way you think, act, and talk. Worst of all, it'll keep you chained to the memories. Forgiving is hard. Forgiving means praying for them. Smart people do stupid stuff. Good people do bad stuff. And misguided people don't know what they are doing (Luke 23:34). You may understand someday. Or you may never understand. Either way, for your own sake, forgive. Hit the delete button and move on.

Glory to God

Now, to Him who is able to keep you from stumbling, And to present you faultless before the presence of His glory with exceeding joy, to God our Savior, who alone is wise, be glory and majesty, dominion and power, both now and forever, amen.

35

The Epistle of Jude 1:24, 25

Let the words of my mouth and the meditation of my heart be acceptable in your sight, O Lord, my Strength and my Redeemer.
Psalm 19:14

Doxology

Praise God, from whom all blessings flow,
Praise Him, all creatures here below,
Praise Him above, ye heav'nly host;
Praise Father, Son, and Holy Ghost.
Amen

God loves you....
For God so loved the world, that He gave His only begotten Son, that whoever believes in Him should not perish but have everlasting life.
John 3:16

But God demonstrates His own love towards us, in that while we were yet sinners, Christ died for us.
Romans 5:8

All are Sinners

For all have sinned and fall short of the glory of God.
Romans 3:23
As it is written: There is none righteous, no, not one.
Romans 3:10

RESPECT FOR THE TRINITY

Ecclesiastes 5 The Source

Let us be mindful of the direction of our thankfulness. When we rise in the morning and see the sunrise, whom do we thank? When we make it home from the day's labor without any hurt, harm, or danger to us, whom do we thank? When we see our children after sending them out to the world as sheep among wolves, whom do we thank? When we get a clean bill of health from the doctor and/or when we come home directly from the courthouse, whom do we thank?

Are we too conflicted in making deals with the devil that we have forgotten to give thanks to the originator? Have we gotten to the point wherein every time we open our mouth, we start to choke on our own lies? Have we gotten to the point, where we think, we only have drive-by leaders, both in the religious and secular segments that we pay no attention to authority? Do we really think that we are pimp proof and player proof? Oh, but by the grace of God...there go I. Are we the lost generation who find every reason and excuse under the sun for not fellowshipping and worshiping the Trinity within a temple? Have the messages become so materialistic that the churches themselves are contributing to family collapses and community catastrophes? Is this one of the reasons we have more of our fathers and sons in prisons than churches, colleges, and universities? Has all of our entertainment disintegrated to violence and pornography?

Then if so, these are some of the reasons why we should go to church. We don't go because we say the church is full of hypocrites. Well aren't we being hypocritical for using that as an excuse for not going?

Haven't the Bible proven itself worthy of our trust? Psalm 88 is very bleak, but it even recognizes God as the source of our light. Do you respect the Trinity enough to say thank you? The highest expression of faith is communal praise. The greatest amount of respect to God is obedience to His word. The greatest sacrifice to be given is the sacrifice of praise.

God rains on the just and the unjust. He favors whom He wants to, and blesses the just and the unjust. Won't you – being just or unjust bless the Lord? The giver and taker of life? He who loves each and every one of us unconditionally.

Where is your faith?

Who are you obedient to?

What are your sacrifices and to who?

For whatever a man sowth that shall he reap.

For God is not mocked.

HAVE RESPECT FOR GOD

Some Final Words: In Conclusion

We are called to live lives and hearts open to His guidance. When we seek His Will and commit to follow Him in everything, we will not miss opportunities to **obey** Him. And our obedience, even in matters that seem trivial, does have eternal consequences. The adversary tempts us with sins that are likely to look and feel good to our physical selves—a habit that gives pleasure or solace is easier to justify than one that seems repulsive. But no sinner is truly happy chasing after wickedness. Authentic joy is found only in a friendship with the Lord. Taking pleasure in the Lord requires that we understand His attitude toward us: Our Father loves us passionately. He sees past our faults and mistakes to the precious child He created. In fact, He loves us so much that He sent Jesus Christ to save our lives and enable us to be with Him in heaven eternally. We have no greater friend.

The Lord is worthy of praise. He is our Friend, our Rock, and our Protector. What's more, He saved us from death! If we let ourselves get caught up in the opinion of others, we could forget that He is the only audience that matters. Ever since creation, the Lord has deserved and received praise offerings for His glory. Don't be fearful or embarrassed. Give God His due. It is a good thing to note—literally—the results of our obedience to God's instructions. Journaling about His provision and the growth of our faith will inspire us to continue adding to our foundation of truth. That means choosing new areas to remodel according to God's blueprint.

Being saved is not about keeping a perfect record of behavior. If we could do that, we wouldn't need the Father's grace. He knows we are human and prone to making selfish choices contrary to His will. When we do, Jesus Christ acts as our Advocate, because His sacrifice is what makes possible our relationship with the Father.

Next time you pray, start with words of praise to God for His sacrificial love, (1John 4:10-11) [In this is love, not that we loved God, but that He loved us and sent His Son to be the propitiation for our sins. Beloved, if God so loved us, we also ought to love one another.]; and gratitude to Jesus for dying in your/my place. Express that you/we/I understand why your/our prayers are heard—because you/we have a relationship with the Father through Christ, and not because of anything we have done. Confess all known and unknown sins and ask for forgiveness. Then present your requests to God faithfully, that He will answer. The moment you confess your need for Him, something will happen inside you. The Lord will begin to make His presence known. Whether you are age seven or seventy-seven tell Jesus, "Lord I need you. I can't do this without You." You will never lose the eternal gift He gives to you through **faith in** His Son. He takes full responsibility for your need as you **obey** His commands. Our part is to make Him top Priority, and then all these things shall be added unto us (Matt.6:33). This is a promise. He has all the wisdom, power, and ability necessary to fulfill His promises, and He is utterly faithful to His Word (Isaiah 46:11).

The Model Prayer
The Lord's Prayer
Book of Matthew: chapter 6 v. 9-15

In this manner, there, pray:
Our Father in Heaven,
Hallowed be Your name.
Your kingdom come.
Your will be done.
On earth as it is in heaven.
Give us this day our daily bread.
And forgive us our debts,
As we forgive our debtors.
And do not lead us into temptation.
But deliver us from the evil one.
For Yours is the kingdom, and the power and the glory forever.
Amen.
For if you forgive men their trespasses, your heavenly Father will also forgive men their trespasses, as will your Father forgive your trespasses.

The Names of the Books of the Bible Along with Their Abbreviations and Chapters
New Testament

MATTHEW	Mt	28			
MARK	Mk	16			
LUCK	Lk	24			
JOHN	Jn	21			
ACTS OF THE APOSTLE	Acts	28	1st JOHN	1Jn	5
ROMANS	Rom	16	2nd JOHN	2Jn	1
1st CORINTHIANS	1Cor	16	3rd JOHN	3Jn	1
2nd CORINTHIANS	2Cor	13	JUDE	Jude	1
GALATIANS	Gal	6	REVELATION	Rv	22
EPHESIANS	Eph	6			
PHILIPPIANS	Phil	4			
COLOSSIANS	Col	4			
1st THESSALONIANS	1Thes	5			
2nd THESSALONIANS	2Thes	3			
1st TIMOTHY	1Tm	6			
2nd TIMOTHY	2Tm	4			
TITUS	Ti	3			
PHILEMON	Phlm	1			
HEBREWS	Heb	13			
JAMES	Jas	5			
1st PETER	1Pt	5			
2nd PETER	2Pt	3			

The Names of the Books of The Bible Along with Their Abbreviations and Number of Chapters
Old Testament

GENESIS	Gn	50			
ECCLESIASTES	Eccl	12			
SONG OF SONGS	Sg	8			
EXODUS	Ex	40	WISDOM *	wis	19
LEVITICUS	Lv	27	SIRACH*	Sir	51
NUMBERS	Nm	6	ISAIAH	Is	66
DEUTERONOMY	Dt	34	JEREMIAH	Jer	52
JOSHUA	Jos	24	LAMENTATIONS	Lam	5
JUDGES	Jgs	21	BARUCH *	Bar	6
RUTH	Ru	4	EZEKIEL	Ez	48
1st SAMUEL	1Sm	31	DANIEL	Dn	14
2nd SAMUEL	2Sm	24	HOSEA	Hos	14
1st KINGS	1Kgs	22	JOEL	Jl	4
2nd KINGS	2Kgs	25	AMOS	Am	9
1st CHRONICLES	1Chr	29	OBADIAH	Ob	1
2nd CHRONICLES	2Chr	36	JONAH	Jon	4
EZRA	Ezra	10	MICAH	Mi	7
NEHEMIAH	Neh	13	NAHUM	Na	3
TOBIT*	Tb	14	HABAKKUK	Hb	3
JUDITH *	Jdt	16	ZEPHANIAH	Zep	3

ESTHER		Est	10	HAGGAI	Hg	2
1st MACCABEES *		1Mc	16	ZECHANIAH	Zec	14
2nd MACCABEES*		Mc	15	MALACHI	Mal	3
JOB	Jb	42		Footnote***These chapters are in the New American		
PSALMS	Ps(s)	150		Bible for Catholics		
PROVERBS	Prv	31				

THE TEN COMMANDMENTS
Book of Exodus Chapter 20
Book of Deuteronomy Chapter 5

I.   You shall have no other gods before Me.

II. You shall not make for yourself a carved image—any likeness of anything that is in heaven above, or that is in the earth beneath, or that is in the water under the earth; you shall not bow down to them nor serve them. The Lord will show mercy to thousands, to those who love Me and keep My commandments.

III. You shall not take the name of the Lord your God in vain, for the Lord will not hold him guiltless who takes His name in vain.

IV. Remember the Sabbath day, to keep it holy. Six days you labor and do all your work, but the seventh day is the Sabbath of the Lord your God.

V.   Honor your father and your mother, as the Lord your God has commanded you, that your days may be long.

VI. You shall not murder.

VII. You shall not commit adultery.

VIII.You shall not steal.

IX.. You shall not bear false witness against your neighbor.

X.   You shall not covet your neighbor's wife, house, field, servant, or anything that is your neighbor's.

THE GREAT 'NEW' COMMANDMENTS

"Which is the great commandment in the law?" Jesus said to him, "You shall love the Lord your God with all your heart, with all your soul, and with all your mind." This is the first and great commandment. And the second is like it: "You shall love your neighbor as yourself. On these two commandments hang all the Law and the Prophets."

Try Something Different

When you greet one another in the morning, noonday, or evening:
Saying "Good Morning" is so ritual, so mundane, and so unmeaningful. It's just going through the motions.
How about saying: Happy Monday…
Let's get personal. How about we say: Have a Marvelous Monday or Have a Magnificent Monday.
Can you come up with one? What about…
Have a terrific Tuesday.
Have a wonderful Wednesday.
Have a thankful Thursday.
Have a fantastic Friday.
Have a sensational Saturday.
Have a spiritual Sunday.
What do you think?
I like it. Do you?

The Twelve of Jesus Apostles (Disciples)

1. Simon Peter—Fisherman
2. Andrew—Simon's brother
3. James
4. John
5. Levi (Matthew) a tax collector
6. Philip
7. Bartholomew
8. Thomas
9. James (Son of Alphaeus)
10. Simon (Zealot)
11. Judas (Son of James)
12. Judas Iscariot

The Golden Rule

Matthew 7:12
In everything, do to others what you would have them do to you, for this sums up the Law and the Prophets.

The Story of the Twelve Tribes of Israel

When Abram was ninety-nine (99) years old, the Lord appeared to Abram and said to him, "I am Almighty God; walk before Me and be blameless. And I will make My covenant between Me and you, and will multiply you exceedingly." Then Abram fell on his face, and God talked with him, saying: "As for Me, behold, My covenant is with you, and you shall be a father of many nations. No longer shall your name be called Abram, but your name shall be Abraham; for I have made you a father of many nations. I will make you exceedingly fruitful; and I will make nations of you, and Kings shall come from you. And I will establish My covenant between Me and you and your descendants after you in their generations, for an everlasting covenant, to be God to you and your descendants after you. Also I give to you and your descendants after you the land in which you are a stranger, all the land of Canaan, as an everlasting possession, and I will be their God." And God said to Abraham: "As for you, you shall keep my covenant, you and your descendants after you throughout their generations," (Gen. 17: 1-9).

Then God said to Abraham, "As for Sarai your wife, you shall not call her name Sarai, but Sarah shall be her name. And I will bless her and also give you a son by her; then I will bless her, and she shall be a mother of nations, kings of peoples shall be from her," (Gen. 17: 15-16).

"Sarah your wife shall bear you a son, and you shall call his name Isaac. I will establish my covenant, and with his descendants after him. And as for Ishmael, I have heard you. Behold, I have blessed him, and will make him fruitful, and will multiply him exceedingly. He shall beget twelve princes, and I will make him a great nation. But My covenant I will establish with Isaac, whom Sarah shall bear to you at this time next year," (Gen.17: 19-21).

And Abraham called the name of his son who was born to him—whom Sarah bore to him—Isaac. Then Abraham circumcised his son Isaac when he was eight days old, as God had commanded him. Now Abraham was one hundred years old when his son Isaac was born to him (Gen.21: 3-5).

Now this is the genealogy of Ishmael, Abraham's son, whom Hagar the Egyptian, Sarah's maidservant, bore to Abraham. And these were the names of the sons of Ishmael, by their names, according to their generations: The first born of Ishmael, Nebajoth; then Kedar, Adbeel, Mibsam, Mishma, Dumah, Massa, Hadar, Tenna, Jetur, Naphish, and Kedemah. These were the sons of Ishmael and these were their names, by their towns and their settlements, twelve princes according to their nations. These were the years of the life of Ishmael: one hundred and thirty seven years, and he breathed his last and died, and was gathered to his people (Gen. 25:12-17).

Isaac was forty years old when he took Rebekah as wife. Now Isaac pleaded with the Lord for his wife, because she was barren; and the Lord granted his plea, and Rebekah his wife conceived. But the children struggled together within her; and she said, "If all is well, why am I like this?" So she went to inquire of the Lord. And the Lord said to her: "Two peoples shall be separated from your body: One people shall be stronger than the other, and the older shall serve the younger." So when her days were fulfilled for her to give birth, indeed there were twins in her womb. And the first came out red. He was like a hairy garment all over; so they called his name Esau. Afterward his brother came out, and his hand took hold of Esau's heel; so his name was called Jacob. Isaac was sixty years old when she bore them (Gen.25:20-28).

The story continues in the book of Genesis. Please, find time to read the entire book of Genesis. Esau ends up selling his birthright to Jacob, which causes Esau to lose his birthright, There after comes a famine in the land and the Lord appears to Isaac and tells Isaac what 'land to dwell in and that He will be with Isaac and bless him and his descendants. God tells Isaac that He will "make his descendants multiply as the stars of heaven. That in his seed all the nations of the earth shall be blessed; because Abraham obeyed My voice and kept My charge, My commandments, My statues, and My laws."

Isaac ends up blessing Jacob whom he thought was Esau due to the fact that his eyes had gone bad and he was in his golden age years. So not only did Jacob end up with Esau's birthright, but he also got Esau's blessing with the help of his mother, Rebekah (Don't forget to read the story for detail clarification, including Jacob's obedience to this mother). Jacob felt that his father would know he was not his brother and he became a deceiver to him. He thought he would bring a curse on himself instead of a blessing (Gen.27:12). But showing a mother's love for her son, Rebekah said to him, "Let your curse be on me, my son, only obey my voice." So in essence, Jacob's obedience to his mother caused him to deceive his father, thus receiving the blessing intended for Esau. Isaac blessing Jacob made Jacob master of Esau and all his brother's servants to Jacob, thus manifesting the word of God spoken to Rebekah right before she gave birth. So when Isaac finally blessed Esau, his blessing was that he "shall live by the sword and serve his brother. And it shall come to pass when you(Esau) become restless, that you shall break his yoke from your neck."

Jacob had to escape from Esau. Esau hated Jacob with a passion and sought to kill him. Isaac continued to bless Jacob that God Almighty blessed him to be fruitful and multiply that he became an assembly of people and inherited the blessing of Abraham.

After Jacob's escape, he married Leah and Rachel. Between Leah and Rachel and the maidservants, they bore him twelve sons and one daughter (Gen. 30).

How did the name of **Israel** come about for the twelve tribes?

Jacob is the third great ancestor of the people of Israel. His name was changed to Israel when he struggled with God at Peniel near the Jabbok River. And it is written: Jacob said, "I will not let you go unless You bless me!" And the Man whom Jacob wrestled with said to him, "What is your name?" He said "Jacob." And He said, "Your name shall no longer be called Jacob, but Israel: for you have struggled with God and with men, and have prevailed." And God blessed him.

Jacob's Twelve Sons

Remember Jacob had two wives...The sons of Leah were: Reuben, Simeon, Levi, Judah, Issachar, and Zebulun. The sons of Zilpah (Leah's maidservant) were Gad and Asher. The sons of Rachel were Joseph and Benjamin. The sons of Bilhah (Rachel's maidservant) were Dan and Naphtali.

Thus were the twelve (12) tribes of Israel for whom much land was distributed among themselves and their descendants. Esau's descendants also received much land.

A Quote or Two

Determination makes the difference in getting something done.
　　　　– excerpt from *Acknowledgements*, Kay Allenbaugh, p.252

What we are is God's gift to us. What we become is our gift to God.
　　　　– author unknown p.54

You can let the same force that makes flowers grow and planets move run your life, or you can do it yourself
　　　　– *Divine Assistance* p.43, by Marianne Williamson

Life is either a daring adventure—or nothing.
　　　　– p.90, Helen Keller

Peace is seeing a sunset and knowing whom to thank.
　　　　– p.63 author Unknown

For something new to begin, something must end.
　　　　– Crossroads, p.128—Kris King

Aspire to inspire before you expire.

Pushing through our fears and self-doubt can be a prolonged process; or a simple decision.
　　　　– p.192 by Linda Blackman

The way I see it, if you want the rainbow, you gotta put up with the rain
　　　　– Dolly Parton

Changing the way we perceive incidents in our life can change the way we respond to them.
> – p.204 (Grace) Jennifer James

We are created equal, yet we seldom die that way.... Where you end up is up to you.... If you think there is something good in everybody...you haven't met everybody.
> – The Vent 2/8/2008

You can trap a lie...but you can't trap the truth.
> – *City Café*/Jan. 2004 Security Guard

MY DECISION TO RECEIVE CHRIST
AS MY SAVIOR

CONFESSING TO GOD THAT I AM A SINNER AND BE-
LIEVING THAT THE LORD JESUS CHRIST DIED FOR
MY SINS ON THE CROSS AND WAS RAISED FROM THE
DEAD FOR MY JUSTIFICATION, I DO NOW RECEIVE
AND CONFESS HIM AS MY PERSONAL SAVIOR

NAME_____

DATE_____

SEEKING A CHURCH

AFTER MAKING YOUR DECISION TO RECEIVE CHRIST, I ENCOURAGE YOU TO PRAYERFULLY SEEK A LOCAL CHURCH, CONGREGATION, OR ASSEMBLY THAT WILL ASSIST YOU IN GROWING AS A NEW CHRISTIAN BY THE CLEAR TEACHING OF THE BIBLE.

CONTINUE TO GROW IN THE GRACE AND KNOWLEDGE OF OUR LORD AND SAVIOR JESUS CHRIST
II PETER 3:18

IF YOU ENJOYED THIS BOOK…YOU WILL ENJOY THE SPIRIT FILLED BOOK TO COME: "THE FRUIT OF THE SPIRIT: DO YOU POSSESS THEM…………..GAL 5:22-23

Epilogue

Remember, when you research and study God's word, be mindful to view not only the King James Version, but also the Living Bible or the New International Version. Never forget to pray before you read. Prayer will bring God's spirit to lead you to an understanding of what you are reading.

For example, one evening, I was reading the Book of Acts chapter nineteen, from the eleventh through the twentieth verses; the contents were about God working miracles through the hand of Paul in the name of our Lord Jesus Christ. I did not fully discern what it was saying as I read the New International Version. The Holy Spirit uttered to me to go downstairs and get The New American Bible. This version translated fully for me what I had read, and I comprehended exactly what those verses were saying. There were some additional Jews trying to cast out evil spirits in the name of Paul.

One God, One Faith, One Baptism

I say that to say "God the Father, God the Son, and God the Holy Ghost."

There are many versions of the Bible available. Certainly, there is one to suit your fancy. I have extracted various verses for our edification in His Word from the diverse collection I have been privileged to come across.

Now mind that there are many religions and theologies…historical realities vs. historical myths…but contrarily, there is still only one yesterday, today, and tomorrow.

One Lord

One Faith

One Baptism

Eph. 4:5

The Holy Trinity: God the Father, God the Son, God the Holy Spirit.

Blessed be the name of the Lord

References (Bibliography)

The Book of Mormon
 "Another testament of Jesus Christ," 1981 published by The Church of Jesus Christ of Latter-Day Saints, Salt Lake City, Utah, USA

The New King James Version of The Holy Bible
 1982 by The American Bible Society

The New International Version of The Holy Bible
 1984 by The International Bible Society

He Did it All for You
 By Kenneth and Gloria Copeland. 2005 published by Kenneth Copeland Publications 1-800-600-7395

Mankind's Search for God
 Watch Tower Bible (1990) and Tract Society of Pennsylvania

From Fear to Faith
 Merlin Carothers, Thomas Nelson Publishers 1997 Nashville, Tn.

Prison to Praise
 1970 by Merlin Carothers

Adult Christian Life
 R.H. Boyd Publishing, 1st Qtr. 2006